Cassowary Coast

Count Back Crocodile

Written by
Pamela Galeano

Illustrated by
Dorothy Webster (Mirrimum)

Cassowary Coast - Count Back Crocodile
First published 2013

National Library of Australia Cataloguing -in- Publication entry.

Author:	Galeano, Pam, author.
Title:	Count back crocodile / written by Pamela Galeano ; illustrator, Dorothy Webster (Mirrimum).
Series:	Galeano, Pam Cassowary coast ; No 2.
Notes:	Includes bibliographical references.
ISBN:	9780980494747 (paperback)
Target Audience:	For pre-school age.
Subjects:	Counting--Juvenile literature.
	Crocodiles--Juvenile literature.

Other Authors/Contributors: Webster, Dorothy, illustrator
Dewey Number: 513.211

Illustrations by Dorothy Webster, rendered in acrylic on paper
Prepress & layout by Daryl Dickson, Wildcard Art
Text of this book in Arial

Printed by Boolarong Press

Author's Dedication

For all the Indigenous residents of the Cassowary Coast

Illustrator's Dedication

For my Grandparents, Thomas Barclay-Miller
and
Grandma Nora

We wish to thank Jirrbal Elder Uncle Ernie Grant and Girramay Elder Aunty Marcia Jerry for sharing their knowledge of Aboriginal language.

ten 10

10

yunggul bulayi balan bulayi-bulayi

(yung´gul bul´ay bulan bul ´ay bul´ay)

Ten little hatchlings
Floating in a line
Mother Monitor grabs her lunch
Now there are nine.

Bevan

nine 9

9

balan gariburr-gariburr

(bulan ´garriburr ´garriburr)

Nine hungry hatchlings
Smelling tasty bait
One is unlucky
Now there are eight.

Bevan

eight 8

8

balan yunggul bulayi-bulayi

(bulan yung´gul bul´ay bul´ay)

Eight silly hatchlings
Head for the Bevan
Thinking it’s their mum - ‘Help!’
Now there are seven.

seven 7

balan bulayi-bulayi 7

(bulan bul´ay bul´ay)

Seven clever hatchlings
Practising new tricks
Barramundi snaps one up
Now there are six.

six 6

gariburr gariburr 6

(´garriburr ´garriburr)

Six frisky hatchlings
Learning how to dive
It's Sea Eagle's dinner time
Now there are five.

five 5

yunggul bulayi-bulayi 5

(yung ´gul bul´ay bul´ay)

Five happy hatchlings
Gobble larvae raw
Heron spies a bigger meal
Now there are four.

four 4

bulayi - bulayi 4

(bul ´ay bul ´ay)

Four hatchlings hide
Beneath a mangrove tree
But Water Rat comes sniffing
Now there are three.

three 3

balan 3

(bulan)

Three fearful hatchlings
Sense a danger new
Water Python needs a feed
Now there are two.

two 2

bulayi 2

(bul ´ay)

Two chilly hatchlings
Basking in the sun
But Jabiru’s out hunting
Now there’s only one.

one 1

yunggul 1

(yung´gul)

One little hatchling
Believes his learning done
Mud Crab finds him under slime
Now there are none.

zero 0

But Bevan’s dad
Arrives on cue
He knows exactly
What to do

Again there are two!

How Maui found his Father and the Magic Jawbone

Peter Gossage

MAUI WAS HAPPY he had found his mother Taranga.
But two things bothered him.
Who was his father?
And where did his mother go during the day?